THE BOOKS OF THE BIBLE

My Bible Story
Coloring Book

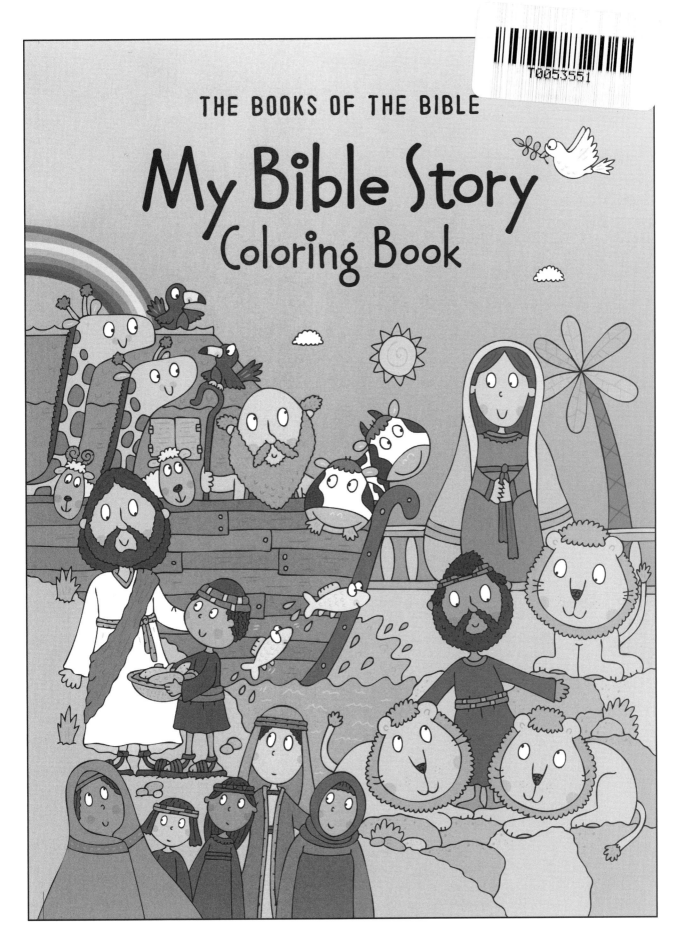

Table of Contents

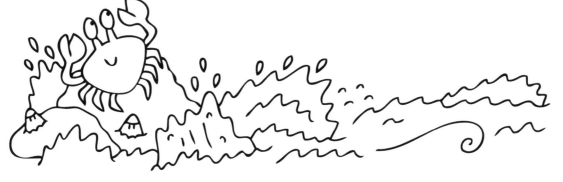

Covenant History

Week 1

Noah's Ark

The Lord saw how bad the sins of everyone on earth had become. So God said to Noah, "I am going to put an end to everyone. They have filled the earth with their harmful acts. I am going to destroy them and the earth. So make yourself an ark out of cypress wood. I am going to bring a flood on the earth. Everything on earth will die. But I will make my covenant with you. You will go into the ark. Your sons and your wife and your sons' wives will enter it with you. Two of every kind of bird will come to you. Two of every kind of animal will also come to you. And so will two of every kind of creature that moves along the ground. All of them will be kept alive with you."

Noah did everything just as God commanded him.

For 40 days the flood kept coming on the earth. As the waters rose higher, they lifted the ark high above the earth. After 40 days Noah opened a window he had made in the ark. Then he sent out the dove from the ark. In the evening the dove returned to him. There in its beak was a freshly picked olive leaf! So Noah knew that the water on the earth had gone down.

Noah came out of the ark. His sons and his wife and his sons' wives were with him. All the animals came out of the ark, one kind after another.

The LORD said to himself, "I will never put a curse on the ground again because of human beings. I will never destroy all living things again, as I have just done. The rainbow is the sign of my covenant. I have made my covenant between me and all life on earth."

Joseph and the Colorful Robe

Joseph was a young man. He was 17 years old. Israel loved Joseph more than any of his other sons. Israel made him a beautiful robe. Joseph's brothers saw that their father loved him more than any of them. So they hated Joseph. They couldn't even speak one kind word to him.

Joseph had a dream. When he told it to his brothers, they hated him even more. He said to them, "Listen to the dream I had. We were tying up bundles of grain out in the field. Suddenly my bundle stood up straight. Your bundles gathered around my bundle and bowed down to it."

His brothers said to him, "Do you plan to be king over us? Will you really rule over us?" So they hated him even more because of his dream.

Joseph's brothers had gone to take care of their father's flocks. Joseph went to look for his brothers. But they saw him a long way off. Before he reached them, they made plans to kill him.

"Here comes that dreamer!" they said to one another. "Come. Let's kill him. Let's throw him into one of these empty wells. Let's say that a wild animal ate him up. Then we'll see whether his dreams will come true."

When Joseph came to his brothers, he was wearing his beautiful robe. They took it away from him. And they threw him into the well.

They saw some Ishmaelite traders coming from Gilead.

Judah said to his brothers, "What will we gain if we kill our brother? Let's sell him to these traders." Judah's brothers agreed with him.

The traders sold Joseph to Potiphar in Egypt. Potiphar put Joseph in prison. While Joseph was there, the LORD was with him. He gave Joseph success in everything he did.

When years had passed, Pharaoh had a dream. In his dream, he was standing by the Nile River. Seven cows came up out of the river. They looked healthy and fat. After them, seven other cows came. They looked ugly and skinny. The ugly, skinny cows ate up the seven cows that looked healthy and fat. Then Pharaoh woke up.

In the morning no one could tell him what they meant. So Pharaoh sent for Joseph. He was quickly brought out of the prison. Pharaoh said to Joseph, "I had a dream. No one can tell me what it means. But I've heard that when you hear a dream you can explain it."

"I can't do it," Joseph replied to Pharaoh. "But God will give Pharaoh the answer he wants."

Joseph said, "Seven years with plenty of food are coming to Egypt.

14

But seven years when there won't be enough food will follow them.

"So Pharaoh should look for a wise man. He should put him in charge of Egypt. They should collect all the extra food of the good years that are coming. It will be needed during the seven years when there isn't enough food."

Pharaoh said to Joseph, "God has made all this known to you. No one is as wise as you are. You will be in charge of my palace."

Joseph's brothers went down to Egypt to buy grain there. There wasn't enough food in the land of Canaan. Joseph was the governor of the land. He was the one who sold grain to all its people. When Joseph's brothers arrived, they bowed down to him with their faces to the ground. Joseph said to his brothers, "I am Joseph!" But his brothers were afraid of him.

Joseph said, "Come close to me." So they did. Then he said, "I am your brother Joseph. I'm the one you sold into Egypt. But don't be upset. God sent me ahead of you to save many lives."

Joseph kissed all his brothers and wept over them. After that, his brothers talked with him.

The news reached Pharaoh's palace that Joseph's brothers had come. Pharaoh said to Joseph, "Tell your brothers, 'Load your animals. Return to the land of Canaan. Bring your father and your families back to me. I'll give you the best land in Egypt. You can enjoy all the good things in the land.'"

Week 3
Moses and the Burning Bush

Moses came to Horeb. It was the mountain of God. There the angel of the LORD appeared to him from inside a burning bush. Moses saw that the bush was on fire. But it didn't burn up.

God spoke to him from inside the bush. He called out, "Moses! Moses!"

"Here I am," Moses said.

"Do not come any closer," God said. "Take off your sandals. The place you are standing on is holy ground."

The LORD said, "I have seen how my people are suffering in Egypt. I have heard them cry. I have come down to save them from the Egyptians. I will bring them up out of that land. I will bring them into a good land. It is a land that has plenty of milk and honey. So now, go. I am sending you to Pharaoh. I want you to bring the Israelites out of Egypt. They are my people."

But Moses spoke to God. "Who am I that I should go to Pharaoh?" he said.

God said, "I will be with you. I will give you a sign. It will prove that I have sent you." The LORD said to him, "What do you have in your hand?"

"A walking stick," he said.

The LORD said, "Throw it on the ground."

So Moses threw it on the ground. It turned into a snake. Then the LORD said to Moses, "Reach your hand out. Take the snake by the tail." So he reached out and grabbed the snake. It turned back into a walking stick in his hand. The LORD said, "When they see this sign, they will believe that I appeared to you."

Week 4
Moses and the Fiery Lawgiving

Here are the rules and laws I'm announcing to you today. Learn them well. Be sure to obey them. The LORD our God made a covenant with us at Mount Horeb. He didn't make it only with our people of long ago. He also made it with us. In fact, he made it with all of us who are alive here today. The LORD spoke to you face to face. His voice came out of the fire on the mountain. At that time I [Moses] stood between the LORD and you. I announced to you the LORD's message. I did it because you were afraid of the fire. You didn't go up the mountain.

Later on, your child might ask you, "What is the meaning of the terms, rules and laws the LORD our God has commanded you to obey?" If they do ask you, tell them, "We were Pharaoh's slaves in Egypt. But the LORD used his mighty hand to bring us out of Egypt. The LORD our God commanded us to obey all his rules. He commanded us to honor him. If we do, we will always succeed and be kept alive."

The LORD chose you because he loved you very much. He wanted to keep the promise he had made to your people of long ago. That's why he used his mighty hand to bring you out of Egypt. He bought you back from the land where you were slaves. He set you free from the power of Pharaoh, the king of Egypt.

Week 5

Rahab and the Spies

Joshua sent two spies from Shittim. He sent them in secret. He said to them, "Go and look over the land. Most of all, check out Jericho." So they went to Jericho. They stayed at the house of Rahab.

The king of Jericho was told, "Look! Some of the Israelites have come here tonight. They've come to check out the land."

But the woman had hidden the two men. She had taken them up on the roof. There she had hidden them under some flax she had piled up. The king's men left to hunt down the spies.

Rahab went up on the roof before the spies settled down for the night. She said to them, "The LORD your God is the God who rules in heaven above and on the earth below. Promise me in the name of the LORD that you will be kind to my family. I've been kind to you."

So the men made a promise to her. "If you save our lives, we'll save yours," they said. "Just don't tell anyone what we're doing. Then we'll be kind and faithful to you when the LORD gives us the land."

The house Rahab lived in was part of the city wall. So she let the spies down by a rope through the window. She said to them, "Go up into the hills. The men chasing you won't be able to find you. Hide yourselves there for three days until they return. Then you can go on your way."

Week 6
David and Goliath

The Philistines gathered their army together for war. A mighty hero named Goliath came out of the Philistine camp. He was more than nine feet tall.

Goliath stood there and shouted to the soldiers of Israel. He said, "Why do you come out and line up for battle? Choose one of your men. Have him come down and face me." Saul and the whole army of Israel heard what the Philistine said. They were terrified.

David reached the camp as the army was going out to its battle positions. The soldiers were shouting the war cry.

David said to Saul, "Don't let anyone lose hope because of that Philistine. I'll go out and fight him."

Saul replied, "You aren't able to go out there and fight that Philistine. You are too young. He's been a warrior ever since he was a boy."

But David said to Saul, "The LORD saved me from the paw of the lion. He saved me from the paw of the bear. And he'll save me from the powerful hand of this Philistine too."

Then David picked up his wooden staff. He went down to a stream and chose five smooth stones. He put them in the pocket of his shepherd's bag. Then he took his sling in his hand and approached Goliath.

Goliath looked David over. He saw how young he was. And he hated him. He said to David, "Why are you coming at me with sticks? Do you think I'm only a dog?"

David said to Goliath, "You are coming to fight against me with a sword, a spear and a javelin. But I'm coming against you in the

name of the LORD who rules over all. He is the God of the armies of Israel. He's the one you have dared to fight against."

As the Philistine moved closer to attack him, David ran quickly to the battle line to meet him. He reached into his bag. He took out a stone. He put it in his sling. He slung it at Goliath. The stone hit him on the forehead and sank into it. He fell to the ground on his face.

So David won the fight against Goliath with a sling and a stone. He struck down the Philistine and killed him. He did it without even using a sword.

King Solomon's Riches

The queen of Sheba heard about how famous Solomon was.
She also heard about how he served and worshiped the LORD.
So she came to test Solomon with hard questions. She arrived in
Jerusalem with a very large group of attendants. Her camels were
carrying spices, huge amounts of gold, and valuable jewels. She
came to Solomon and asked him about everything she wanted to
know. Solomon answered all her questions.

There wasn't anything too hard for the king to explain to her. So the queen of Sheba saw how very wise Solomon was. She saw the palace he had built. She saw the food on his table. She saw his officials sitting there. She saw the robes of the servants who waited on everyone. She saw his wine tasters. And she saw the burnt offerings Solomon sacrificed at the LORD's temple. She could hardly believe everything she had seen.

She said to the king, "Back in my own country I heard about how much you had accomplished. I also heard about how wise you are. So I came to see for myself. And now I believe it! You are twice as wise and wealthy as people say you are. The report I heard doesn't even begin to tell the whole story about you. How happy your people must be! How happy your officials must be! They always get to serve you and hear the wise things you say. May the LORD your God be praised. He takes great delight in you. He placed you on the throne of Israel. The LORD will love Israel for all time to come. That's why he has made you king. He knows that you will do what is fair and right."

Week 8
Elijah Goes to Heaven

Elijah and Elisha were on their way from Gilgal. The LORD was going to use a strong wind to take Elijah up to heaven.

So the two of them walked on. A group of men faced the place where Elijah and Elisha had stopped at the Jordan River. Elijah rolled up his coat. Then he struck the water with it. The water parted to the right and to the left. The two of them went across the river on dry ground.

After they had gone across, Elijah said to Elisha, "Tell me. What can I do for you before I'm taken away from you?"

"Please give me a double share of your spirit," Elisha replied.

"You have asked me for something that's very hard to do," Elijah said. "But suppose you see me when I'm taken away from you. Then you will receive what you have asked for. If you don't see me, you won't receive it."

They kept walking along and talking together. Suddenly there appeared a chariot and horses made of fire. The chariot and horses came between the two men. Then Elijah went up to heaven in a strong wind. Elisha saw it and cried out to Elijah, "My father! You are like a father to me! You, Elijah, are the true chariots and horsemen of Israel!" Elisha didn't see Elijah anymore.

Prophets

Jonah and the Huge Fish

The LORD said, "Go to the great city of Nineveh. Preach against it." But Jonah ran away from the LORD. He sailed for Tarshish.

The LORD sent a wild storm. The ship was in danger of breaking apart. The sailors were afraid. Each cried out to his own god.

But Jonah had gone below deck. He lay down and fell into a deep sleep. The captain went to him and said, "How can you sleep? Get up. Call to your god for help."

The sea was getting rougher. So the sailors asked Jonah, "What should we do to make the seas calm down?"

"Pick me up and throw me into the sea," he replied. "Then it will become calm. It's my fault that this terrible storm has come on you." Instead of doing what he said, the men did their best to row back to land. But they couldn't. The sea got even rougher than before.

Then they threw Jonah overboard. The stormy sea became calm. When the men saw that, they began to have great respect for the LORD. But the LORD sent a huge fish to swallow Jonah.

Jonah was inside the fish for three days and three nights. From inside the fish Jonah prayed to the LORD. The fish spit Jonah up onto dry land. Jonah obeyed the LORD. He went to Nineveh.

Week 2

Wolves with Lambs

Wolves will live with lambs.
Leopards will lie down with goats.
Calves and lions will eat together.
And little children will lead them around.
Cows will eat with bears.
Their little ones will lie down together.
And lions will eat straw like oxen.

49

A baby will play near a hole where cobras live.
A young child will put its hand into a nest
where poisonous snakes live.

None of those animals will harm or
destroy anything or anyone
on my holy mountain of Zion.
The oceans are full of water.
In the same way, the earth will be filled
with the knowledge of the LORD.

Week 3

I Will Give Them a Sign

"I will give them a sign. I will send to the nations some of those who are left alive. And I will send still others to islands far away. The people who live there have not heard about my fame. They have not seen my glory. But when I act, those I send will tell the nations about my glory. And they will bring back all the people of Israel from all those nations. They will bring them to my holy mountain in Jerusalem.

My people will ride on horses, mules and camels. They will come in chariots and wagons," says the LORD. "Those messengers will bring my people as an offering to me. They will bring them to my temple, just as the Israelites bring their grain offerings in bowls that are 'clean.' And I will choose some of them to be priests and Levites," says the LORD.

"I will make new heavens and a new earth. And they will last forever," announces the LORD. "In the same way, your name and your children after you will last forever. Everyone will come and bow down to me. They will do it at every New Moon feast and on every Sabbath day," says the LORD.

Week 4

People of Zion, Sing!

People of Zion, sing!
Israel, shout loudly!
People of Jerusalem, be glad!
Let your hearts be full of joy.
The LORD has stopped punishing you.
He has made your enemies turn away from you.
The LORD is the King of Israel.
He is with you.

You will never again be afraid
that others will harm you.
The time is coming when people
will say to Jerusalem,
"Zion, don't be afraid. Don't give up.

The LORD your God is with you.
He is the Mighty Warrior who saves.
He will take great delight in you.
In his love he will no longer punish you.
Instead, he will sing for joy because of you."

Week 5

You Will Be My People

The LORD says,

"I will bless Jacob's people with great success again.

I will show tender love to Israel.

Jerusalem will be rebuilt where it was destroyed.

The palace will stand in its proper place.

From those places the songs of people giving thanks will be heard.

The sound of great joy will come from there.

I will cause there to be more of my people.

There will not be fewer of them.

I will bring them honor.

People will have respect for them.

"Things will be as they used to be for Jacob's people.
I will make their community firm and secure.
I will punish everyone who treats them badly.
Their leader will be one of their own people.
Their ruler will rise up from among them.
I will bring him near.
And he will come close to me.
He will commit himself to serve me,"
announces the LORD.
"So you will be my people.
And I will be your God."

Week 6

Vision of Ezekiel

I looked up and saw a windstorm coming from the north. I saw a huge cloud. The fire of lightning was flashing out of it. Bright light surrounded it. The center of the fire looked like glowing metal. I saw in the fire something that looked like four living creatures. They appeared to have the shape of a human being. But each of them had four faces and four wings. Their legs were straight. Their feet looked like the feet of a calf. They were as bright as polished bronze. The creatures had human hands under their wings on their four sides. Each of the four creatures had the face of a human being. On the right side each had the face of a lion. On the left each had the face of an ox. Each one also had an eagle's face. The living creatures looked like burning coals of fire or like torches. Fire moved back and forth among the creatures. It was bright. Lightning flashed out of it. The creatures raced back and forth like flashes of lightning.

Then a voice came from above the huge space over their heads. They stood with their wings lowered. Above the space over their heads was something that looked like a throne made out of lapis lazuli. On the throne high above was a figure that appeared to be a man. From his waist up he looked like glowing metal that was full of fire. From his waist down he looked like fire. Bright light surrounded him. The glow around him looked like a rainbow in the clouds on a rainy day.

That's what the glory of the LORD looked like. When I saw it, I fell with my face toward the ground.

Week 7
The Valley of Dry Bones

The power of the LORD came on me. His Spirit brought me away from my home. He put me down in the middle of a valley. It was full of bones. The bones were very dry. The LORD asked me, "Son of man, can these bones live?"

I said, "LORD and King, you are the only one who knows."

Then he said to me, "Prophesy to these bones. Tell them, 'Dry bones, listen to the LORD's message. The LORD and King speaks to you. He says, "I will put breath in you. Then you will come to life again. I will attach tendons to you. I will put flesh on you. I will cover you with skin. So I will put breath in you. And you will come to life again. Then you will know that I am the LORD."'"

So I prophesied just as the LORD commanded me to. As I was prophesying, I heard a noise. It was a rattling sound. The bones came together. One bone connected itself to another. I saw tendons and flesh appear on them. Skin covered them. But there was no breath in them.

Then the LORD said to me, "Prophesy to the breath. Prophesy, son of man. Tell it, 'The LORD and King says, "Breath, come from all four directions. Go into these people who have been killed. Then they can live."'" So I prophesied just as he commanded me to. And breath entered them. Then they came to life again. They stood up on their feet. They were like a huge army.

Week 8

I Will Return to Zion

A message came to me from the LORD who rules over all.

"I will return to Zion. I will live among my people in Jerusalem. Then Jerusalem will be called the Faithful City. And my mountain will be called the Holy Mountain."

He continued, "Once again old men and women will sit in the streets of Jerusalem. All of them will be using canes because they are old. The city streets will be filled with boys and girls. They will be playing there."

He continued, "All of that might seem hard to believe to the people living then. But it will not be too hard for me."

He continued, "I will save my people. I will gather them from the countries of the east and the west. I will bring them back to live in Jerusalem.

They will be my people. I will be their faithful God. I will keep my promises to them."

Writings

Week 1

The Shepherd's Psalm

The LORD is my shepherd. He gives me everything I need.

He lets me lie down in fields of green grass.

He leads me beside quiet waters.

He gives me new strength.

He guides me in the right paths for the honor of his name.

Even though I walk through the darkest valley,

I will not be afraid.

You are with me.

Your shepherd's rod and staff comfort me.

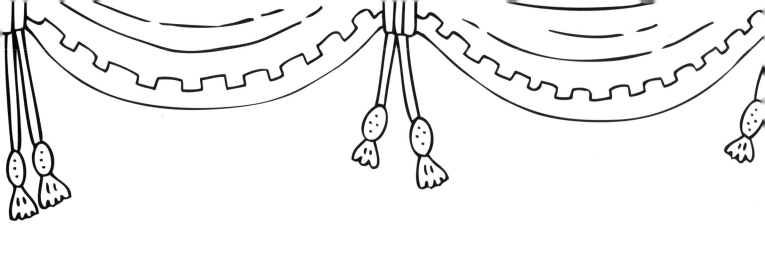

You prepare a feast for me right in front of my enemies.
You pour oil on my head.
My cup runs over.

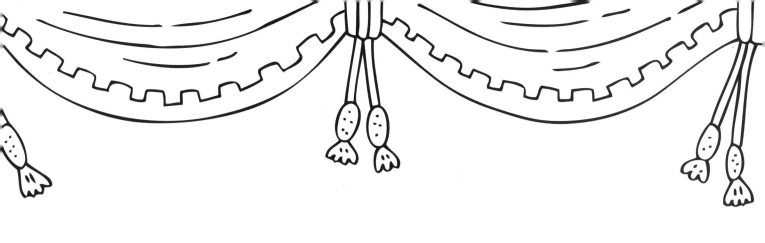

Your goodness and love will follow me all the days of my life.

And I will live in the house of the LORD forever.

Week 2
Sparrow Near the Altar

LORD who rules over all,

    how lovely is the place where you live!

I can't wait to be in the courtyards of the LORD's temple.

    I really want to be there.

My whole being cries out

    for the living God.

LORD who rules over all,

    even the sparrow has found a home near your altar.

My King and my God,

    the swallow also has a nest there,

    where she may have her young.

Blessed are those who live in your house.

    They are always praising you.

Blessed are those whose strength comes from you.

    They have firmly decided to travel to your temple.

As they pass through the dry Valley of Baka,

    they make it a place where water flows.

    The rain in the fall covers it with pools.

Those people get stronger as they go along,
   until each of them appears in Zion, where God lives.
Lord God who rules over all, hear my prayer.
   God of the people of Jacob, listen to me.
God, may you be pleased with your anointed king.
   You appointed him to be like a shield that keeps us safe.
A single day in your courtyards is better
   than a thousand anywhere else.
I would rather guard the door of the house of my God
   than live in the tents of sinful people.
The Lord God is like the sun that gives us light.
   He is like a shield that keeps us safe.
   The Lord blesses us with favor and honor.
He doesn't hold back anything good
   from those whose lives are without blame.
Lord who rules over all,
   blessed is the person who trusts in you.

Week 3

Psalm 121

I look up to the mountains.
Where does my help come from?
My help comes from the LORD.
He is the Maker of heaven and earth.
He won't let your foot slip.
He who watches over you won't get tired.
In fact, he who watches over Israel
won't get tired or go to sleep.
The LORD watches over you.

The LORD is like a shade tree at your right hand.

The sun won't harm you during the day.

The moon won't harm you during the night.

The LORD will keep you from every kind of harm.

He will watch over your life.

The LORD will watch over your life no matter where

you go,

both now and forever.

Week 4

What is a Proverb?

These are the proverbs of Solomon. He was the son of David and the king of Israel. Proverbs teach you wisdom and instruct you. They help you understand wise sayings.

They provide you with instruction and help you live wisely. They lead to what is right and honest and fair.

They give understanding to childish people. They give knowledge and good sense to those who are young.

Let wise people listen and add to what they have learned. Let those who understand what is right get guidance.

What I'm teaching also helps you understand proverbs and stories.

It helps you understand the sayings and riddles of those who are wise.

If you really want to gain knowledge, you must begin by having respect for the LORD.
But foolish people hate wisdom and instruction.

Trust in the LORD with all your heart.
Do not depend on your own understanding.

In all your ways obey him.
Then he will make your paths smooth and straight.

Week 5

The Story of Job

There was a man who lived in the land of Uz. His name was Job. He was honest. He did what was right. He had respect for God and avoided evil. One day angels came to the LORD. Satan also came with them. The LORD said to Satan, "Where have you come from?"

Satan answered, "From traveling all around the earth. I've been going from one end of it to the other."

Then the LORD said to Satan, "Have you thought about my servant Job? There isn't anyone on earth like him. He is honest. He does what is right. He has respect for God and avoids evil."

"You always give Job everything he needs," Satan replied. "That's why he has respect for you. Haven't you guarded him and his family? Haven't you taken care of everything he has? You have blessed everything he does. His flocks and herds are spread all through the land. But now reach out your hand and strike down everything he has. Then I'm sure he will speak evil things against you. In fact, he'll do it right in front of you."

The LORD said to Satan, "All right. I am handing everything he has over to you. But do not touch the man himself."

Then Satan left the LORD and went on his way. He sent painful sores on Job. They covered him from the bottom of his feet to the top of his head. He got part of a broken pot. He used it to scrape his skin. He did it while he was sitting in ashes.

His wife said to him, "Are you still continuing to be faithful to the LORD? Speak evil things against him and die!"

Job replied, "You are talking like a foolish woman. We accept good things from God. So we should also accept trouble when he sends it."

In spite of everything, Job didn't say anything that was sinful. After Job had prayed for his friends, the LORD made him successful again. He gave him twice as much as he had before. All his brothers and sisters and everyone who had known him before came to see him. They ate with him in his house. They showed their concern for him. They comforted him because of all the troubles the LORD had brought on him. Each one gave him a piece of silver and a gold ring.

The LORD blessed the last part of Job's life even more than the first part.

Week 6

Building the Temple

Solomon began to build the temple of the LORD. He built it on Mount Moriah in Jerusalem. That's where the LORD had appeared to Solomon's father David.

Solomon laid the foundation for God's temple. It was 90 feet long and 30 feet wide. The porch in front of the temple was 30 feet across and 30 feet high.

Solomon covered the inside of the temple with pure gold. He decorated the hall with palm tree patterns and chain patterns. He decorated the temple with valuable jewels. He covered the ceiling beams, door frames, walls and doors of the temple with gold. He carved cherubim on the walls.

He built the Most Holy Room. It was 30 feet long and 30 feet wide. He covered the inside of the Most Holy Room with 23 tons of fine gold. He also covered the upper parts with gold.

The gold on the nails weighed 20 ounces. For the Most Holy Room, Solomon made a pair of carved cherubim. He covered them with gold.

Week 7

Josiah Celebrates Passover

Josiah celebrated the Passover Feast in Jerusalem to honor the LORD. The Passover lamb was killed on the 14th day of the first month. Josiah appointed the priests to their duties. The Levites taught all the people of Israel. The Levites had been set apart to the LORD. Josiah said to them, "Put the sacred ark of the covenant in the temple Solomon built." Josiah provided animals for the Passover offerings. He gave them for all the people who were there. He gave a total of 30,000 lambs and goats and 3,000 oxen. His officials also gave freely. They gave to the people and the priests and Levites.

The guards at each gate didn't have to leave their places. That's because their brother Levites got things ready for them. So at that time the entire service to honor the LORD was carried out. The Passover Feast was celebrated. The burnt offerings were sacrificed on the LORD's altar. That's what King Josiah had ordered. The Israelites observed the Feast of Unleavened Bread for seven days.

The Passover Feast hadn't been observed like that in Israel since the days of Samuel the prophet. None of the kings of Israel had ever celebrated a Passover Feast like Josiah's. He celebrated it with the priests and Levites. All the people of Judah and Israel were there along with the people of Jerusalem. He celebrated it with them too.

Week 8

Daniel and the Lions' Den

Daniel went home to his upstairs room. Its windows opened toward Jerusalem. He went to his room three times a day to pray. He got down on his knees and gave thanks to God. Some men saw him praying. They said to the king, "Didn't you sign an order? For the next 30 days no one of your people could pray to any god except you. If they did, they would be thrown into the lions' den." The king answered, "The order must be obeyed." The men spoke again: "Daniel doesn't obey the order. He still prays to God."

So the king gave the order. Daniel was brought out and thrown into the lions' den. The king said to him, "May God save you."

The king returned to his palace. He didn't eat anything that night. He couldn't sleep. As soon as the sun began to rise, the king got up. He hurried to the lions' den.

When he got near it, he called out to Daniel, "Daniel! You serve the living God. Has he been able to save you from the lions?"

Daniel answered, "My God sent his angel. And his angel shut the mouths of the lions. They haven't hurt me at all." The king was filled with joy. He ordered his servants to lift Daniel out of the den.

New Testament

Week 1

Angel Visits Mary and Jesus is Born

God sent the angel Gabriel to a virgin. The girl was engaged to a man named Joseph. The virgin's name was Mary. The angel said, "The Lord is with you." Mary was very upset. But the angel said, "Do not be afraid, Mary. God is pleased with you. You will give birth to a son. You must name him Jesus."

"How can this happen?" Mary asked. The angel answered, "The Holy Spirit will come to you. The holy one that is born will be called the Son of God. Nothing is impossible with God."

"I serve the Lord," Mary answered. "May it happen to me just as you said it would." Then the angel left her.

Caesar Augustus required that a list be made of everyone in the whole Roman world. All went to their own towns to be listed.

Joseph went to Bethlehem, the town of David. He went there with Mary. Mary was engaged to him. She was expecting a baby.

While Joseph and Mary were there, the time came for the child to be born. She gave birth to her first baby. It was a boy. She wrapped him in large strips of cloth. Then she placed him in a manger. There was no room for them in the inn.

Week 2

The Road to Damascus

Saul wanted to find men and women who belonged to Jesus. He wanted to take them as prisoners to Jerusalem.

On his journey, Saul approached Damascus. Suddenly a light from heaven flashed around him. He fell to the ground. He heard a voice say to him, "Saul! Saul! Why are you opposing me?"

"Who are you, Lord?" Saul asked.

"I am Jesus," he replied. "I am the one you are opposing. Now get up and go into the city. There you will be told what you must do." The men traveling with Saul weren't able to speak. They heard the sound. But they didn't see anyone.

Saul got up from the ground. He opened his eyes, but he couldn't see. So the men led him by the hand into Damascus. For three days he was blind.

In Damascus there was a believer named Ananias. The Lord called to him in a vision, "Ananias! Go to the house of Judas on Straight Street. Ask for a man named Saul. He is praying."

Then Ananias went to the house. He placed his hands on Saul. "Brother Saul," he said, "you saw Jesus. He has sent me so that you will be able to see again. You will be filled with the Holy Spirit."

Right away something like scales fell from Saul's eyes. And he could see again. He got up and was baptized.

Week 3

The Glory of God

I, Paul, am writing this letter. I have been chosen to be an apostle of Christ Jesus just as God planned. Our brother Sosthenes joins me in writing.

We are sending this letter to you, the members of God's church in Corinth. God has chosen you to be his holy people. He has done the same for all people who pray to our Lord Jesus Christ. Jesus is their Lord and ours.

May God our Father and the Lord Jesus Christ give you grace and peace.

I am free and don't belong to anyone. But I have made myself a slave to everyone. I do it to win as many as I can to Christ. I do all this because of the good news. And I want to share in its blessings. So eat and drink and do everything else for the glory of God.

Don't do anything that causes another person to trip and fall. It doesn't matter if that person is a Jew or a Greek or a member of God's church. Follow my example. I try to please everyone in every way. I'm not looking out for what is good for me. I'm looking out for the interests of others. I do it so that they might be saved.

Week 4

God's Armor

Finally, let the Lord make you strong. Depend on his mighty power. Put on all of God's armor. Then you can remain strong against the devil's evil plans. Put the belt of truth around your waist. Put the armor of godliness on your chest. Wear on your feet what will prepare you to tell the good news of peace.

Also, pick up the shield of faith. With it you can put out all the flaming arrows of the evil one. Put on the helmet of salvation. And take the sword of the Holy Spirit. The sword is God's word.

Week 5
Jesus Feeds the Multitude

Jesus saw a large crowd. He felt deep concern for them. He healed their sick people.

When it was almost evening, the disciples came to him. They said, "It's already getting late. Send the crowds away. They can go and buy some food in the villages."

Jesus replied, "They don't need to go away. You give them something to eat."

"We have only five loaves of bread and two fish," they answered.

"Bring them here to me," he said.

Then Jesus directed the people to sit down on the grass. He took the five loaves and the two fish. He gave thanks. He broke the loaves into pieces. Then he gave them to the disciples. And the disciples gave them to the people.

All of them ate and were satisfied. The disciples picked up 12 baskets of leftover pieces. The number of men who ate was about 5,000. Women and children also ate.

The Last Supper and Crucifixion

The day came to celebrate the Passover Feast. Jesus sent out two of his disciples. He told them, "Go into the city. A man carrying a jar of water will meet you. Follow him. He will show you a large upstairs room. Prepare for us to eat there."

The disciples went into the city. They found things just as Jesus had told them.

So they prepared the Passover meal. When evening came, Jesus arrived with the Twelve.

While they were eating, Jesus took bread. He gave thanks and broke it. He handed it to his disciples and said, "Take it. This is my body."

Then he took the cup. He gave thanks and handed it to them. All of them drank from it.

"This is my blood poured out to forgive the sins of many," he said. Then they sang a hymn and went out to the Mount of Olives.

Jesus and his disciples went to Gethsemane. Jesus said, "Sit here while I pray." Judas came, guiding a group of soldiers. They were carrying torches and weapons. Jesus asked them, "Who is it that you want?"

"Jesus of Nazareth," they replied.

"I am he," Jesus said.

Then the soldiers arrested Jesus. Then they handed him over to Pilate.

"Are you the king of the Jews?" asked Pilate.

"Yes. It is just as you say," Jesus replied.

Pilate handed Jesus over to be nailed to a cross. Jesus had to carry his cross to a place called the Skull. There the soldiers nailed him to the cross. Jesus died.

Week 7

The Empty Tomb

A rich man named Joseph took Jesus' body and wrapped it in a clean linen cloth. He placed it in his own new tomb. He rolled a big stone in front of the tomb. Pilate put a seal on the stone and placed some guards on duty.

Mary Magdalene and the other Mary went to look at the tomb. They saw that the stone had been rolled away. They entered the tomb. As they did, they saw an angel dressed in a white robe. The angel said to the women, "Don't be afraid. I know you are looking for Jesus. He is not here! He has risen, just as he said! Go! Tell his disciples and Peter." So the women hurried away from the tomb, they were afraid, but they were filled with joy. They ran to tell the disciples.

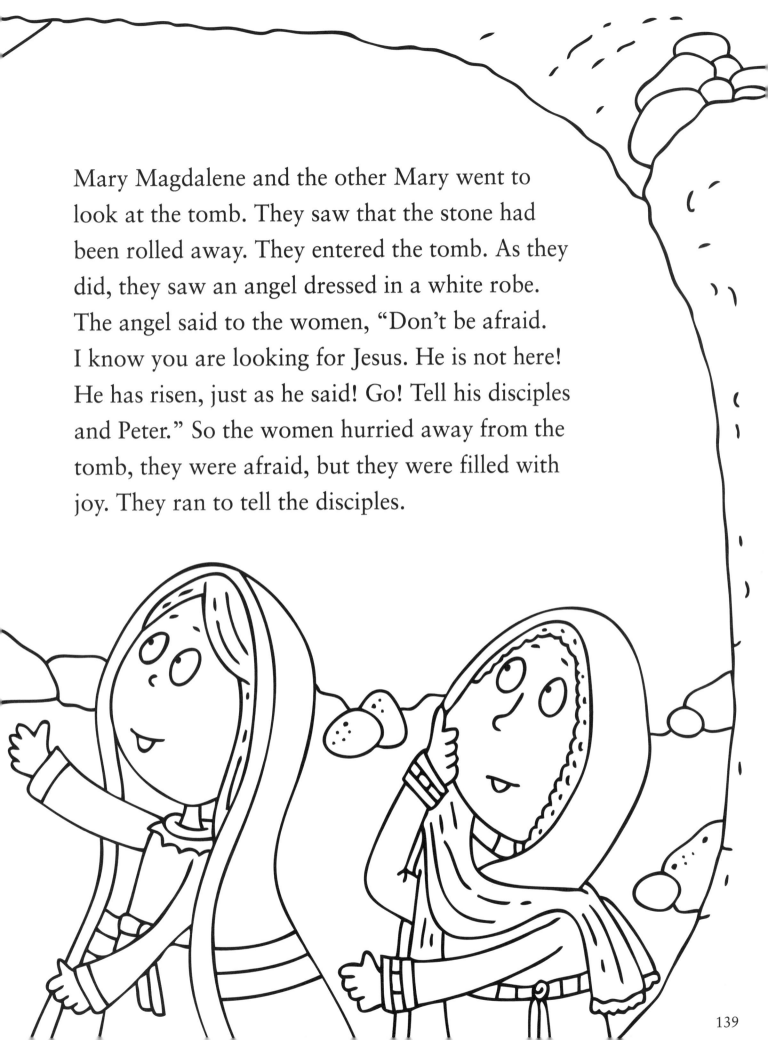

Week 8

Streets of Gold

The angel carried me away in a vision. The Spirit took me to a huge, high mountain. He showed me Jerusalem, the Holy City. It was coming down out of heaven from God. It shone with the glory of God. The city had a huge, high wall with 12 gates. Twelve angels were at the gates. The wall was made out of jasper. The city was made out of pure gold. The foundations of the city walls were decorated with every kind of jewel. I didn't see a temple in the city. That's because the Lamb and the Lord God who rules over all are its temple.

Then the angel showed me the river of the water of life. It was as clear as crystal. It flowed from the throne of God and of the Lamb. It flowed down the middle of the city's main street. The throne of God and of the Lamb will be in the city. God's servants will serve him. Then he told me, "Look! I am coming soon! I bring my rewards with me. I will reward each person for what they have done. I am the First and the Last. I am the Beginning and the End. Anyone who is thirsty should come. Anyone who wants to take the free gift of the water of life should do so. Jesus is a witness about these things. He says, "Yes. I am coming soon."

Amen. Come, Lord Jesus!

May the grace of the Lord Jesus be with God's people. Amen.

ZONDERKIDZ

My Bible Story Coloring Book
Copyright © 2017 by Zondervan
Illustrations © 2017 by Zondervan

Published in Grand Rapids, Michigan, by Zonderkidz. Zonderkidz is a registered trademark of The Zondervan Corporation, L.L.C., a wholly owned subsidiary of HarperCollins Christian Publishing, Inc.

Requests for information should be addressed to customercare@harpercollins.com.

ISBN 978-0-310-76106-8

Editor: Barbara Herndon
Illustrations: Simon Abbott
Design: Cindy Davis

Printed in United States of America

24 25 26 27 28 /CWR/ 13 12 11 10